He was "the best at his position that I ever saw."

- Ray Nitschke - quote from 1962

"As a boy I admired Dan Currie's abilities and wanted to emulate him. Little did I know I'd be playing his position one day and it would earn me a place in the Hall of Fame."

- Dave Robinson

"I knew Dan from Michigan State. He was a senior when I was a sophomore. We became friends in Green Bay. He's a great football player, a fine man and one of the beautiful people."

- Herb Adderley

"Danny? I loved the hell out of him."

- Paul Hornung

"Fun to be a movie star but it never compares to being a football star...never."

~ Burt Reynolds

Movie (2017) - The Last Movie Star

The Packers' number one draft choice in 1958, Dan Currie was a steady performer at outside linebacker for seven seasons in Green Bay. The former Michigan State Spartan Star, nicknamed "Dapper Dan," he intercepted 11 passes, recovered six fumbles and returned an interception for a touchdown during his Packer career.

The 6'3", 240-pound Currie played on the 1961 and '62 NFL championship teams and was All-Pro after each of those seasons. He was a member of the Packers from 1958-'64.

(Courtesy - Packers Hall of Fame.)

2019-2020 by Sandy Sullivan. All rights reserved.
No part of this book may be reproduced, stored in a retrieval system, or
transmitted by any means, electronic, mechanical, photocopying, recording, or
otherwise, without written permission from the author.

Dapper Dan's Diary

The Fascinating Personal Account of an

All-American

- First Round Draft Pick -

Green Bay Legend

DAN CURRIE

Compiled By

Sandy Sullivan

(This text is written just as I told it to my friend, Sandy Sullivan.)

Dan Currie – 2009 – Milwaukee

Dedication

This book is for
my teammates, friends, fans,
for young, aspiring athletes
and my children.

Dan Currie

Dapper Dan's Diary

From the written words of

Dan Currie

beginning in 1971 at age 36.

Chapter 1

- First of All -

A career in sports has no tangible beginning. You suddenly start swinging a bat, throwing a ball, skating on wobbly ankles or running with a football, all at once. You're growing up. You're excited about your beautiful young life. The bumps and bruises don't bother you.

You begin to understand what winning is all about. You win and then you win again and then you lose and you discover you don't like losing.

All the while you're throwing the ball; throwing it better and better. You're hitting the ball harder and running faster and with more power than most of the other kids. Your body develops and the other kids start looking up to you and you realize you're a bit different from them but you are not sure why or how.

This comes together for most athletes and then the day arrives when you realize you have to work harder to achieve new standards of excellence. You get into organized sports and you fall into eager hands who want to groom you and then things really start to happen.

That would pretty much summarize the youth of most athletes, regardless of how far their sports career extends. But I think as a kid growing up on the Eastside of Detroit in the 1940's, there were a number of other factors which gave me an early advantage in sports.

-MY YOUTH WAS BLESSED WITH CHILDHOOD JOY, FUN AND GAMES-

Our neighborhood had enough kids to organize any type of seasonal sport there was. It was great! We had a large but somewhat bumpy vacant lot right near my home where we battled and played. Of course the tall grass had to be cut with our parents' lawn mowers and the holes had to be filled and the mounds leveled. But all of us worked together to make it playable and after that we would mark the field with out of bounds lines and/or whatever, to make it as "official" as possible.

We were great imitators. If any of us had been to a baseball game that day at what was then Briggs Stadium to see the Tigers play, we would come back to *our* field and try to re-create, as best we could, some of the better plays we had just seen performed by the professionals.

I would try to emulate "Skeeter" Webb at shortstop in making a double play or wind up like the "Little T from Tennessee," Tommy Bridges, though my curve ball never broke anywhere near his round house.

Each of us had someone to imitate. We were all acting as we slid into a base, fielded a grounder, caught a pop up or swung a bat.

It took no time at all before we got into trouble when we started to hit the ball pretty good. Of course we had to paint the home run distances on the houses that faced left and right field. That little mark of graffiti plus several broken windows caused a "rhubarb" and put a slight damper on our eager athletic competition.

-RECALLING EVEN TINY DETAILS FROM AGE SIX-

I was the third of the four boys in our family. My brother Archie was 16 and he was tall and handsome and his own man. Archie could do everything and was a leader in the neighborhood.

My brother Miles, 14, was starting high school and he too was starting to show signs of great potential; academically as well as in sports.

I was six years old and my brother Michael was just a baby.

We were all deeply devoted to our parents; at least I knew how much I was. My mother was a beautiful woman who had a delightful sense of humor. She was Polish and came from All-Polish Hamtramek, a central city. She and my father met while they were working in a factory.

We had a very happy home and we boys joined in with our

parents who liked to sing and dance. They had a lot of friends with whom they socialized or entertained at home. They were hardy, not heavy drinkers; my dad loved his beer and my mom, in her typical Polish way, would order a shot and a beer but it always seemed that she was the one doing the escorting on the way home; which meant she kept my father from bouncing off the walls. You could hear them singing and laughing from blocks away and the neighbors absolutely loved them.

Although he would never admit it, my father was quite possessive and jealous when it came to his pretty wife. He would be very stern with his fellow Irish drinking buddies whenever any one of them stepped out of line with my mother and he did whatever necessary to protect her from jerks.

One hot day, on her way home, my mom stopped off at a local tavern and bought herself a cold beer to cool off. All the people in the bar were friends of mom and dad except for one guy. He was just sitting there by my mom, not even talking to her, when my dad stopped in and dad walked over and decked him. He walked out without saying a word to anyone.

After that, mom never stopped in by herself.

One day, Archie and my dad really went after one another and they flew right out the front door, swinging. My mother was hysterical, crossing herself with holy water from a font near our front door as she mumbled the sign of the cross in Polish. Archie and dad were pounding each other and rolling over and over on the front lawn. I was watching the excitement through the window and my eyes were as big as saucers.

Suddenly my dad dropped him and Archie got up, shook dad's hand and they walked back into the house arm and arm, laughing. Archie said, "Well you won, Dad!"

I'll never forget it! I was six.

-

-Everybody said I was a pretty baby. The next door lady, Mrs. Gobel, called me "China Doll." I couldn't yet say Gobel, so I would call her "Mrs. Go-Go."-

- My Big Brother ARCHIE -
aka "BABY" CURRIE

He was the oldest and Archie was the pride and joy of my parents. He was eager to support himself and always seemed to have provided his own spending money from odd jobs here and there.

Now he was working at the Towne Theater, a nearby movie house, where he was both ticket taker and usher.

One night shortly after midnight, he was leaving the theater to come home. Right around the corner, the Detroit police were having a shoot-out with four hold-up men. It all happened very quickly. Somebody ran toward the theater, a cop fired, and Archie caught a .38 slug right into an ear and dropped dead.

The first thing the next morning, I was awakened and told to go with my father. It was very early and when I got in the back seat of the car I was sleepy and tried to lie down. My brother, Miles, was sitting in the front seat with my dad, who was driving. When we got to the corner of East Grand Boulevard and Charlevoix and stopped for a red light, I saw my father slump over the steering wheel, sobbing. I didn't know what was happening.

My dad was a Detroit fireman, and when we reached the firehouse where he worked, I suddenly felt happy because every time we went there I always got a treat of some kind; like a sandwich, a piece of pie or something good. But as soon as we got there my dad quickly disappeared with a couple of his buddies into a back room and Miles and I we were left sitting there and I still didn't know anything about what was happening.

It was late that afternoon when the coffin with Archie's body was carried into our living room. The entire family was gathered around. All my aunts were there, screaming, sobbing, dropping into chairs and onto the floor, clinging to one another.

One of my aunts tried to crawl into the coffin with Archie, who was so handsome, lying there in a new, dark blue suit. My uncles, who had been drinking with dad in the kitchen, were called in and they had to drag her away.

I didn't cry because I had never experienced anything like this, so I just watched everyone with fascination.

That evening our priest arrived to lead the rosary, and then after most of our friends had left, things really got *hot*. Accusations were thrown around about who was to blame for Archie's staying out so late and working at the movie house.

Why wasn't someone there to meet him and take him home? If someone had been there, he would still be alive. Why did he have to walk home by himself? Where were his friends/the family?

Relatives were looking to put the blame on somebody. They went over the details again and again, looking for reasons, looking in vain for some negligent party to blame for this unbelievable tragedy.

My Aunt Dorothy, a bar maid, probably took Archie's death as hard as anyone. She had been at work at the East Town Bar at Harper and Van Dyke, a few blocks from the movie house and just as she was locking up, a customer ran in and said a young boy had been accidentally killed on the corner. She guessed immediately it was Archie. She was right.

My mom was in severe shock, although I didn't know this at the time. I couldn't figure out what was wrong with her. She wasn't paying any attention to my brother, Miles, my baby brother, Michael, or me.

Later I discovered that for one whole week she went through the motions of displaying grief but simply did not accept that it was *her* son who had died. She closed up and went into a psychological survival mode.

My dad told me on the day Archie was buried, while my mom and he were walking back to the car, she turned to him and said, "Gee, isn't it a shame that something like this had to happen to *that* young boy."

This all happened in 1941 and of course, our lives were never the same again and mom never recovered from Archie's death. The doctors attributed the shock of his death as the cause of a brain tumor which developed and made her an invalid. *(My mom died on my birthday in June of 1973.)*

CHAPTER 2

- All About Us -

Our house was a frantic one. Even after Archie's death, my parents kept up the ritual of keeping things in order with the three of us boys. They frequently inspected our rooms and stressed neatness, both in our appearance and with our personal things.

They would joke around with us saying how big we were getting, especially our feet. Although mom was 5'5" and dad 5'9", all of us boys eventually grew over 6'1" with Miles towering at 6'6".

Years later I would point to my 14-E shoes and jokingly ask them if they were big enough *yet.*

In growing up we all caused them some financial distress when it came to buying clothes because we grew like beans.

I remember one particularly nice outfit I had. There was this pair of second-hand slacks in good condition and a dress jacket which was brand new and I like the outfit very much.

 One day my dad brought home a boy who was having a lot of emotional problems. He was the son of one of dad's best friends who was somewhat down on his luck. To try and make the kid feel at home, dad gave him my new clothes, which I did not give up willingly.

Dad told me the boy needed them far more than I did. I said I understood but I told myself I hoped to hell he *really, really* needed them because I sure did. My dad even went so far as to take the kid to our dentist.

I recall I took great pride in polishing my shoes and pressing my own clothes. I liked shining my dad's shoes as well and I still like mine to be spit shined.

One night mom and dad were going out *stepping* and were all dressed up. They were happy and were a striking couple. They were standing at the door waiting for their good-bye kisses from me. I kissed mom but then I hesitated. Instead of kissing dad, I reached out and shook his hand. He roared with a hardy laugh and shouted, "It finally happened. He's a man."

We shook hands again and they walked out all the happier.

- Baseball Fever-

I was 11 years old when I started getting into the habit of going to Briggs Stadium about 10:30 in the morning if there was an afternoon game scheduled. That was when the head usher would select boys to fill-in part time, wiping off the seats for the ticket holders. If I got picked and it was a good crowd I'd pick up $5 or $7 and got to see batting practice and sometimes even the game itself.

Of course I lived for the Detroit Tigers who were among the contending teams at the time. There was Doc Cramer, Rudy York, Hank Greenberg, Charley Gehringer, Dick Wakefield and the team's two pitching aces, Hal "The Prince" Newhauser and Paul "Dizzy" Trout.

One day while on my way to the ball park I saw both Prince Hal and Dizzy drive by this one particular corner. A couple of days later, on the same corner they came by again, minutes apart, on their way to the ballpark. Both of them lived in the Chicago Boulevard area according to what the papers said.

A week or so went by until one morning while I was purposely standing on *this* corner, Dizzy stopped for a light and he reached over and rolled down the car window.

"Going to the ballpark?" he hollered out at me.

"Sure am, Diz," I said, trying to control my excitement.

"Well, hop in." he replied.

I found myself in the front seat next to Dizzy Trout, heading for Briggs Stadium.

Suddenly we were pulling into Briggs Stadium and all the kids were waving, shouting and holding out their autograph books, looking at the two of us through the windows. The whole scene *hooked* me and it was one I would never forget.

For that whole summer, there I was, scrambling to that one corner hoping to catch the eye of either Dizzy Trout or Prince Hal and time and again I did and it was my first taste of the big time.

They were always smartly dressed in the latest styles. Here were two superstars in their big cars; Dizzy and Hal – names that everybody knew, faces you'd see in the papers every day, and I was often with them. I wanted to be classy-looking like them.

The one thing that really struck me when I was with them was the crowds running after them, and ordinarily, I would have been out there with the other kids and my autograph book trying to get close.

In the fall, my father always managed to come up with tickets to see the Lions play. In those days there were no standing-room-only crowds and my father, who was a Detroit fireman, knew the guys at the gates and all the ushers and they escorted us inside and found *prime* empty seats for us.

There were some great players around – the Bears had Ken Kavanaugh and George McAfee, who later became an NFL official and there were many others who impressed me.

I watched the pros and how they moved on the field – their little idiosyncrasies, the way they handled themselves in certain situations and I would watch them coming out of the clubhouse after a game, walking tall in a way that made everything around them more exciting.

People were there to get their autographs or to just get closer to them. Even though they were out of their uniforms, they were special in a way in which no one in the crowd around them could measure up.

When football season pushed out our summer vacation and things quieted down, we re-made the field on the vacant lot, building our own goalposts and marking off the side lines and end zones. We played whereby we would try extra points after a touchdown. Of course our equipment was make-shift, but we didn't care and it was probably a miracle no one got seriously hurt during this time. When we were organizing and playing these games as best we could.

During all these years, starting from age 10 and right through high school, our group of guys saw a hell of a lot of professional football, baseball and hockey games. For baseball and football, as I said, we got into the ballpark and stadium for nothing. Hockey cost us ninety cents and somehow we always managed to come up with that, plus a little extra for bus fare and a coke.

It wasn't an everyday occurrence, but I guess we went to some game or another about once a week, depending on the season and I know I collected a lot of bottles to earn the cash I needed.

The sport I liked best and was most challenging to us for many reasons, was hockey. We all shared in the rink preparations and the making of the equipment and creating goals to as near regulation as possible.

One of the guys, Jerry Serowski, whose job it was to sew and make the goalie pads, went on to become a surgeon in Minnesota. He not only made the pads but he also stitched the netting for the goals. Our hockey sticks were not too great or solid because they were two pieces of wood hammers together.

Our hockey idols were the Detroit Red Wings, whose production line of Ted Lindsay, Gordie Howe and Sid Abel was the most popular in the National Hockey league, but since I wasn't a free skater, I was most interested in the great goalies of the day: Frank Brimsick of Boston, Turk Broda of Toronto, Bill Durham of Montreal, and, of course Harry Lumley for Detroit.

I zeroed in on the goalies whenever we were up in the rafters of old Olympia Stadium, where for ninety cents we found the best standing-room spots available and for ten cents the bus dropped us off right in front of the stadium.

- My Dilemma with School and the Nuns –

Ours was a devout Catholic family and we lived according to very set traditions. For example, there was never any doubt as to where we would go to school. Saint Anthony's was seven blocks away and my two brothers before me had gone to the grade school and high school there, so, my education, for all 12 years, was plotted out for me. Saint Anthony's would be the focal point for my educational, spiritual and social life.

Saint Anthony's was located right in the middle of the East Side neighborhood where I grew up. It was a mixed, inner-city area with enough kids to get in as much trouble as they could handle or to get involved with as much clean fun and one could stand.

Although ours was far from being a *rough* neighborhood, we had our share of guys who went out looking for trouble but, most all of us loved sports and there were a number of playgrounds, ball diamonds and parks to play in and to watch sandlot baseball, recreational hardball games and whatever. Saint Anthony's itself had great facilities for basket ball, softball and football and they had a field for *night* baseball that was run by the Detroit Department of Parks and Recreation.

-

I guess I could be classified as a non-academic type who achieved very little scholastic success. A running feud with the nuns began the first day I stepped into the first grade classroom and it was a battle that still is talked about in my old neighborhood.

When I was a little kid, I initially thought they just didn't like me, but in later grades they loudly criticized me about how lazy I was in the classroom. They couldn't stand my *lack* of success in the classroom and the *glory* I received on the baseball, football fields and the basketball court.

This kept me honest and tough but thinking back about my lack of success with them, I now realize I was a frustration and they must have felt I was an insult and a reflection of their teaching abilities, although I didn't mean to be.

In second grade I really got barreled by one of the nuns who went at me so damn bad. She pulled me to the front of the class and chewed my ass off.

I was little kid, scared to death, just standing there, embarrassed. All I could see was *red* and from that day on, whenever I got into a tight classroom situation, my brain went blank and I saw colors -- first white, then blue, then *red* and it was really weird.

The nuns were from the tough Notre Dame order and all it took was for one of them to start screaming at me and I went empty.

For all those years their attitude toward me never changed and neither did mine toward them. As a result, I became belligerent and quite unable to take their criticism and I was never able to climb out of the well into which I had fallen.

With each new school year things grew worse and in the seventh grade, when I loved and did well in history, they accused me of having someone write my papers for me and said I was cheating in order to get a good grade.

I never caused any conflict but I battled my way from one classroom to another and I don't know exactly when it began, but gradually I started turning all the hostility which the nuns and I had for one another, into something positive.

I found myself having an additional boost of motivation when I told myself I had to show the nuns how wrong they were about me; I was <u>not</u> *stupid* and I was not a *cheater*.

Day after day that feeling kept building up inside of me and I began doing better and better in sports.

I knew they had to be wrong about me because it was not possible for me to do so poorly in the classroom when in turn, I could react, respond and execute so well on the field and as this battle with the nuns grew more intense, the harder and harder I tried to prove *them* wrong.

Many times over the years I've tried to analyze and understand the breakdown I had with them. I have reasoned that the nuns were never tested in what they were selling. To me, a coach not only gives instruction, but he takes his product -- his team--- out on the avenue and has it publicly tested and measured.

But a teacher can say, *"Oh, he's a slow learner,"* or *"He's uncontrollable,"* and there is no one there to challenge their comments.

From the other side, my side -- as a student -- the more I heard them say statements like this about me, the more and more I was forced backwards, to where it became damn near impossible to catch up with the other students and I really struggled.

When you don't grasp the basics of arithmetic you sure as hell are going to have a difficult time with algebra, geometry and other math courses. Well, that's what was happening to me and I hated it.

I can't recall this conflicting and stressful feeling ever easing up inside me and I was finding it more and more difficult to express myself and learn.

Whenever I had to face a nun, I was stripped of my pride and confidence and then, I would subsequently be sent to the rectory where I'd end up talking to the priest who would try to instill the fear of God in me, and, that did nothing except make we see *red* all over again.

CHAPTER 3

- More Battles –

Nuns vs. Me

From time to time, the nuns would make the obvious comparisons of my academic inability to Miles' accomplishments. He was four years ahead of me and an all-A student. He wound up president of his senior class while also being a fine athlete on the varsity teams of football, basketball and baseball; not outstanding, but a respectable athlete. Of course, that part of the *nun* conflict touched my home because my father, too, didn't understand how Miles could do so well and I couldn't.

When I brought my report card home, I'd ask my mother to sign it so that dad didn't see my grades. Then when he'd corner me, I shrug it off with, "Next time, Dad."

There was no one with whom I could talk over my academic troubles. The nuns could do no wrong as far as my family was concerned and I didn't know where to go to get help. I thought everyone was against me on this front.

- *Then Came My Salvation* -

I was getting more and more active in sports. In the winter months, I went to the gym to play basketball and we stayed until they kicked us out. I felt safe and secure at the gym. I just couldn't get that anxiety out of me any other way or place.

My embarrassment and the stress of not understanding something taught in class evaporated at the gym. I hid my frustrations and didn't share my concerns with anyone and no one probably realized how much I was struggling inside. The gym was a personal sanctuary where I was freed of all that worry.

I was aware that my attitudes were being influenced by athletes, especially as related to their performances on the field. I studied their every move; how they made the big plays, their timing, how they lunged at the ball, how they swung a bat.

By reading the sports pages daily, I was learning and understanding words that described their performances; words like courage, perseverance, and sacrifice. The more I observed and studied their skills on the field, the more I wanted to imitate them. I even noted and practiced the way they popped they fist into a glove, how they tugged at their shirtsleeves before stepping into the batter's box, how they rested their hands on their hips while they stood on a base and watched what was happening in the game.

In ice hockey, I watched the way players would ease up after a big play and slide effortlessly over the ice in a half-crouched position, always keeping their stick parallel to the ice.

In football I watch the way they toned their muscles before a game, clapped their hand when they broke a huddle, or edged up to the scrimmage line before the snap of the ball.

Thousands of little pictures began filling my head and flashing before me as I tried to emulate every move.

I am sure every kid goes through this type of identification or imitation stage in their life, where if one wants to be a singer he listens and watches the moves and expressions of famous singers and so on, but I wanted to be a good athlete and so my focus was on sports and the focus became sharper and sharper every day.

In fourth grade (nine years old) I became an altar boy, which pleased my parents and a few of the nuns. I was told it was an honor and I believed very much that I was close to God while at the altar.

The first time I served mass, I went with the priest to the communion rail as many students were filing down the center aisle to receive. Then I saw my brother Miles taking his turn at the rail and I placed the patent underneath his chin and when he closed his eyes and opened his mouth I nonchalantly said, "Hi Miles," and he almost choked on the host. When we got home that night he kicked the shit out of me and shouted, "Don't you ever embarrass me like that again."

I had memorized a number of stories about the lives of the saints. My grandmother was a grand old gal from Ireland and she liked to hear these stories from me and before she'd doze off she'd look up at me and say, "Daniel, when I get to heaven I'll pray for you and you'll have nothing to worry about, I promise."

-

- Saved by the CYO -

By the time I was in sixth grade I was eligible to compete in the **Catholic Youth Organization** sports program and I had mastered some pretty good skills. Miles had been taking me to see the University of Detroit play their basketball games and to see their star, Norm Swanson, perform. He had this big, high left-handed hook shot.

On Saturdays, when the little squirts got to use the gym, I would practice that hook over and over to where I thought I had it down pretty well. Even though I was right-handed, I thought it made me look darn good throwing that left-handed hook.

Up until the time I started competing in the CYO sports program, I had never given a serious thought about myself, Daniel Currie, being a star or anything else for that matter, and that's because for some reason I was very aware that the rug could be pulled from under you at any time, so I never planned too far ahead. But, as a first-stringer on Saint Anthony's football team in the sixth grade, I remember things changing.

We were playing our first game of the season at the Waterworks Park on Belle Isle, the beautiful island which sits right in the middle of the Detroit River, separating the USA from Canada at that geographical point.

I started at left halfback for Saint Anthony's and on the first series of plays, we had the ball and I ran off left tackle for 37 yards and a touchdown. Then later, I intercepted a pass and ran for another touchdown.

After the game something registered with me. After seeing so many games at Briggs Stadium, I was able to compare my performance that day to the moments of glory I had seen pro athletes experience and I felt I had "something" that would perhaps get me *All-CYO* honors. I wanted those *All-*CYO honors very much and I have always been grateful to that organization for all they did for me and do for so many kids.

In comparison, I knew that my skills and ability were better than the abilities of most of the boys I had been playing with and I have since learned that there is this moment of realization for all star athletes, when they know they are a cut above the rest. That first game gave me a great lift.

The never-ending battle with the nuns was working out more and more to my advantage. Before a game I would purposely recall one or two incidents that had occurred in the classroom that week -- some insult, some degrading remark -- and it would make me so damned mad, I'd get myself all worked up and I'd look forward to knocking off heads on the field of battle.

I was sure if the nuns actually realized what they were doing to my head -- forcing me to become a better athlete -- if they knew I was channeling the anxiety they were causing me -- they might have changed their attitude toward me. They might have even gone to the other extreme and pasted gold stars over everything I owned.

Thus it was sports which became my solution and answer to my silent war with the nuns and the classroom. This was the only way I could prove to them that I wasn't a failure.

However, the more recognition I got, the more difficult the struggle with them became and what eased the pain was my first realization -- my fantasy -- my dream—that if I worked really hard at it, I could *someday* play in Briggs Stadium, too, and I'd show the nuns just how dumb I was!

By the time I reached the eighth grade, I was too big to compete in football, but still eligible to play basketball and baseball. I had perfected that left-handed hook and in general I had a very good year.

We won the CYO City Championship and played before television cameras for the first time. Our basketball opponent in the title game was Jesuit High School and with the help of my 15 points as Saint Anthony's center, we beat them.

ANTHONYS 8TH GRADE C.Y.O. TEAM
49 SOUTHEAST DIVISION CHAMPS.
WON 11 - LOST 2

#10

It took me a few years to grow into my ears.

CHAPTER 4

- Being Seen -

When I was in eighth grade and we played before television cameras for the first time and we won the CYO Detroit Championship in basketball. I scored 15 points as Saint Anthony's center and my mother watched the game on TV and told me how funny we looked coming onto the floor. We had to wear the high school team's warm-up outfits and that meant that the trousers for most of the team were bigger than our whole bodies. But we didn't mind – TV, the winning and all. Yes, indeed, we were top bananas.

Because my mother eventually became an invalid due to the terrible shock of Archie's death, she never saw *me* play any games in person. In fact the only game she ever saw my brother Miles play was the city championship game of 1946 when Saint Anthony's played Cooty High School.

Later in life she would see me on TV and it made me feel good knowing she was watching and that she was proud of me, but my father went to everything.

At the time we played our games in small gyms where the crowds would push right up to the out-of-bounds lines and invariably, when some disputed decision by a ref was made, my dad's hat flew onto the court and I would see him being escorted out of the gymnasium. He was a hell of a loyal fan of Saint Anthony's and of course, his sons.

The disappointment of not being allowed to play football in the eighth grade (because I was too big) was partially eased when John Shoda, the new Saint Anthony's coach, invited me to practice with the high school varsity instead. He took Saint

Anthony's to the city championship that year and he was one of the most talked about coaches in town.

In the sixth and seventh grade we practiced football at the opposite end of the field from the high school players and a priest served as our coach and he drove the team hard, emphasizing fitness more than the technical aspects of the game. His coaching demanded 45 minutes of calisthenics before scrimmaging. No one wore face masks in those days and I was getting used to seeing blood, cuts and bruises. I continued to realize I had some talent, which through hard work, could take me long way.

Our grade school team scrimmaged with another top-notched team in the city that year and one of the best in Michigan -- and I held my own really well.

Most importantly though was the establishment of my relationship with John Shada, one of the most important influences in my life.

Just before I started high school, my brother Miles got married. His wife was also Irish and Polish and they held their reception at one of those club halls used for Polish weddings.

I was in eighth grade and 6'1" and I noticed that being dressed in a tux brought a lot of attention from a number of girls at the wedding.

Four of them cornered me in the bar that evening and they all thought I was in high school...at least. I got so damned nervous, not knowing what to say, or what to do. I just wanted to hide.

I am not sure what I eventually said but it was something like, "Excuse me, girls, I have to go to the bathroom."

Yes, of course, I was mischievous and some childish pranks were inevitable but by today's standards, quite tame.

A young couple lived on the first floor of an apartment building in my neighborhood and one of the guys had seen them in bed together one night. We knew nothing about sex and really didn't know where to go or who to talk to about it. I guess to be more accurate, it was a subject we boys snickered about and were embarrassed to bring out into the open.

One night, in a group, we rode over near their apartment where their bedroom window overlooked the alley. We edged up as close as we could so we could look in.

They never drew the blinds and sometimes there were 10 or 11 bikes parked near the window with their riders watching the show.

But, that's about as far as my nefarious exploits went because I was very fearful of God, my parents, the nuns as well as the priests who instructed us in lessons of morality.

That's how it was growing up in our community and their instruction had a big influence on my athletic career which seemed on the verge of blooming.

CHAPTER 5
- Saint Anthony's -
High School

I stood 6'2" and weighed 190 pounds when I walked into the halls as a freshman at Saint Anthony's High School. The distance from home to school was still the same – seven blocks -- but I got that different vibe and the peculiar feeling that somehow I had arrived at an important juncture in my life.

The nuns and priests in their black habits and cassocks appeared in the hallways and on the school grounds waving, smiling and greeting us.

They all knew who I was and they knew my family and they knew everything about my classroom problems and playing field activities, but even the bitter academic memories couldn't dampen my expectations about high school and playing for John Shada.

Saint Anthony's had hired John Shada the year before and I quickly saw he had a special way about him. He had served in the Pacific in WWII, played service football, traveled and had a relaxed, experienced, confident air about him.

As the basketball coach at the University of Detroit, he had become a popular figure with the sports writers of the city. Now, at Saint Anthony's, he was to coach all three major sports -- football, basketball and baseball -- at a Class B school which had an enrollment of 850 students and right from the beginning he made it clear to me that he expected a great deal from me in the next four years.

From time to time he would throw out such statements as; *"Danny, I'll show you how to get to City Hall,"* *"Danny, I'll get you to Tiger Stadium, just hang in there."*

He was the first of my instructors to give me hope and confidence and someone I felt could and would back up everything he promised.

As a freshman in football, I started as a running back. The two years of organized CYO football and a season of working out with the high school team while I was still in eighth grade, gave me some experience and a certain amount confidence. I was one of five freshmen on the team and we were part of Coach Shada's re-building program after having won the city championship the previous year.

In the opening game against Catholic Central, the largest Catholic high school in the metropolitan area, I tore up my knee. Although no one could figure it out, I was able to play that entire year in all sports with a torn cartilage.

We held our own throughout my freshman year and ended up with a respectable win-loss record, but John Shada's team showed signs of promise and so did I.

In basketball, Coach Shada put me at center. One day he called me aside and showed me a series of photographs that had appeared in *Scholastic Magazine,* put together by Paul Arrison, then the head coach at Villanova University. Below the photos were some valuable tips on how to make the best 12 shots in basketball. Then for 15 minutes a day, Shada made me practice one of those maneuvers until I had pretty much mastered them all.

Again, he had that certain ability of knowing when to push me and when to ease up. He knew he had me to work with for four years, and I knew he had the direct pipeline to all the sports writers in town so that I could get as much publicity as any high school kid in the state of Michigan.

In the opening game of basketball season, I scored six points and we lost. In high school, if the center doesn't score, you don't win. We barely squeezed out a .500 season, but again, we were rebuilding.

The pain in my leg was something terrible and I couldn't take it at times, but I hid it and I managed to finish out the season in both basketball and baseball.

Finally, during the summer vacation, I had my knee operated on; the lateral ligament in my left leg. At the time doctors didn't know much about knee rehab following that kind of operation. I recall one doctor suggesting --

even stressing the point -- that I should *not* run on that leg at all for a couple of months. But I was quite foolish at 15 and I wanted to play ball and within a week I was running the bases, and within a month I was back on the pitching mound throwing as hard as ever.

As it turned out it's a damned good thing that I had all that activity because if I hadn't, there would have been so much atrophy in my leg I probably would have had a very limited career. Even so, my knee would give me trouble for the next 17 years of athletic competition and at times, it still does.

As a sophomore I could feel myself getting stronger but it proved to be a traumatic year. After a good football season, I flunked a subject, my grades were down and I was ruled ineligible to play basketball.

My father berated me publicly and I was all but ostracized by my family. I still went to all the games and cheered for the team. I didn't hide, but I certainly wasn't proud of my status and as a result, I was deprived of that *one* letter in my four years of high school -- the one for that basketball season of my sophomore year and I learned that I had to put in the time studying if I wanted to get to the top.

-

One day my father and I were invited to Yeaman's, a popular and quite expensive restaurant in downtown Detroit. We were guests of a group called the Knife and Fork Club to which the most prominent sports-minded businessmen and political figures belonged.

At the luncheon, my father pointed out Harvey Barkus, a columnist for the Detroit Free Press. "Danny," he said, "that's Harvey Barkus over there. You ought to go over and thank him for the nice article he did on you the other day. He could have written about anyone else, but he picked *you* and made your family very proud."

So I went over to Mr. Barkus and thanked him on behalf of my family. Well, I learned a great lesson about public relations from my father that day. The next day Harvey Barkus wrote a glowing article about Dan Currie, the young athlete who is quite a gentleman. That experience had taught me a lot.

Father-Sons Banquet 1955

Dad, Michael, Me and Miles

Michigan State

DAN CURRIE

CHAPTER 6

- Michigan State - University

In addition to appearances at such gatherings as Father and Son Banquets around the city, I was interviewed not only for newspaper stories, but for radio and television as well.

On one occasion I had been invited to appear on the Bob Murphy Show over WXYX – TV, the ABC affiliate on Detroit, located in the Macabee Building. There was another guest who was scheduled to appear; Vince Banonis, an All-Pro center with the great team of the Chicago Cardinals, who had been an All-American at the University of Detroit under Dutch Clarke. Bononis was now with the Detroit Lions and one of the most popular athletes in town.

In the reception area, he came up to me and introduced himself. He knew about me and congratulated me on my career at Saint Anthony's and asked me about college. I told him I wasn't sure but that I had gotten to know Michigan State pretty well. He was wearing a beautiful double-breasted camel's hair top coat and he smoked a big Churchill-type cigar. We talked before and after the show and he really made an impression on me.

Years after, Vince Banonis and I would always find time to sit down and order a martini or two and talk about our first meeting and how he had become an idol for me as a high school kid who was trying to learn and shape up for college.

I was aware in my senior year of high school that Michigan State had one of the best recruitment teams of coaches and scouts in the country. They were master psychologists and were way ahead of other institutions which were contacting me about athletic scholarships. I had been invited to visit MSU's campus several times and when I got there, whether it was for a football or basketball game, or whether it was just to walk around the campus with someone assigned to me, they treated me royally.

I had also been contacted regularly by representatives from Alabama and Purdue, but when I thought of what I had experienced at Michigan State, I was so indoctrinated by then, it was like going to see my old buddies and this is just what they wanted to accomplish.

One afternoon, while Bill Elias, a prominent Purdue coach, was sitting with me in our living room, my dad interrupted our conversation by calling me into the kitchen where he tried to convince me to try out with the Philadelphia Phillies as a pitcher.

It was a mad house because at the same time, coaches from Alabama were on the telephone wanting to speak with me and to my dad.

Up to this time, I had never talked to anyone from Michigan State about a scholarship and I didn't know if they even wanted me, although I thought they did, but nothing was ever said outright.

That afternoon, for some reason, in all the chaos, I told Bill Elias that I really wanted to go to Michigan State.

"I got something right here in my own backyard that's pretty damn good, I told him.

Then I called the coaches from Alabama -- they were real southern gentlemen -- I mean it -- and I told them of my decision. As it turned out, Alabama didn't win a game in the next four years and that would have been disastrous for my future career as a pro.

A couple of days later, I was finally sure and so I called Duffy

Dougherty and said, "Hi Duffy, this is Dan Currie. I'm coming up!"

"Danny, we will be anxiously awaiting your arrival," he assured me, and, I have quoted that statement many times in my life.

It really never registered with me until I was well settled on the rolling, picturesque campus in East Lansing, just how much of a *selling* job they had done on me to react the way I did when it came time to selecting a college.

I didn't know it at the time but one of Duffy's coaches, Bob Devany, had been assigned to me from the time of my freshmen year in high school. He constantly sent me literature and I was kept really well abreast of how Michigan State was doing, not only in sports but in student government and other activities as well.

Unwittingly, I had been carefully indoctrinated by Bob Devany to "think" **Michigan State** and he obviously did his job very well.

(Note: Regretfully, at this point in the story, this tattered and torn old manuscript which Dan and I began to write in 1971, is missing many of the pages relating to his football career at Michigan State.)

-SSSS

All the good things that were happening to me at Michigan State were being bunched together. Somehow, some way, Duffy Dougherty, the great salesman that he was, managed to have me named **the outstanding college football player in the country**.

And now, appearing on the Ed Sullivan Show was a great honor for every All-American -- but to receive the award from Ed Sullivan himself in front of a huge audience and on live cameras was an unforgettable experience.

Receiving the All–America trophy on the

Ed Sullivan Show.

January, 1958

I stood there, numb, proud, happy, dumbfounded and right at the top of the walk.

Me and my college coach

Duffy Daugherty

After that, the other TV appearances, speaking engagements, meeting important people and the various post-season games in which I would play, were easy to handle.

The first post-season game was game was the north-South game in Montgomery, Alabama. It was one of the four games in which I would serve as co-captain, but the victory went to the South in that first one.

After that was the Hula Bowl in Honolulu, in which I was also a co-captain, but the pros, like Tobin Rote and Elroy Hirsch had us 40-7 at halftime. However, the thrill of going to Hawaii more than made up for this disastrous game.

Then there was the Senior Bowl in Mobile, Alabama where I was once again co-captain and we won the game in the last five seconds when they missed a field goal and soon it was all over; the bowl games, national TV exposure, All-American, Michigan State.

I was drafted by the Green Bay Packers as the number one pick. In looking at the results of the total draft, I saw where the Packers had also selected, Jimmy Taylor, Jerry Kramer and Ray Nitschke and according to many experts it was to be the best draft made by any NFL team. Green Bay had been losing for years and they were given the advantage of the best picks out of the college line-ups.

I went back to school at Michigan State, still recuperating from all the post-season traveling.

The last game for me before reporting to the Packers was to be the College All-Star game in Chicago which was six months away.

At the end of June, I reported to the All-Star camp a couple of days early before the rest of the team got there. They had named me and King Hill co-captains for the game and we had to pose for a lot of pictures and attend a number of luncheons.

The day after all the pictures had hit the newspapers, I received a pleasant surprise, a telegram from my old high school principal:

"Congratulations on your success, Daniel.

Remembering other days and other times.

- Sister Mary Fortunato."

In the All-Star game against the pros, we were playing the Detroit Lions, which had special meaning for me because I had been a Lions fan for a very long time and I had aspired to play in their stadium since I was a little boy and Coach Shada had promised it would happen if I worked hard.

I knew we had only one chance to beat the pros; if things went our way and a couple of the guys got *hot*.

From the opening kick-off, big Alex Karras from Iowa was all over Bobby Layne, the famous Detroit Lion quarterback. Karras dropped him a couple of times and I often wondered how they got along during all the years they were teammates after Alex joined the Lions.

But, the two guys who shared the MVP award were Jim Ninowski, the All-Star quarterback and my Michigan State Spartan teammate and Bobby Mitchell, the speedy wide receiver from the University of Illinois.

Bing, Bing, Bing! Three touchdown passes from Ninowski to Mitchell and we were ahead

21-0 at halftime. We held on in the second half and won going away, 35-19.

WOW! In the locker room after the game, we had one hell of a celebration that carried on into the night.

We were all happy guys, practically everyone with a pro-contract in their hand, going to all parts of the country, and I was packing to join the Packers in Green Bay.

(Some names we all now recognize were playing in this All-America line-up)

1957 All-America Team Ends

- **Jim Phillips**, Auburn (AAB, AFCA, AP-1, FWAA, INS-1, NEA-1, SN, UP-1, Time, WC)

- **Dick Wallen**, UCLA (AAB, AFCA, AP-1, FWAA, INS-1, NEA-1, UP-2, Time, WC)
- Jim Gibbons, Iowa (FWAA, INS-2, SN, AP-3, UP-1)
- Fred Dugan, Dayton (FWAA, AP-2)
- Les Walters, Penn State (AP-2)
- Dave Kaiser, Michigan State (UP-2)
- Dick Lasse, Syracuse (INS-2)
- Gary Kapp, Utah State (INS-2)
- Don Ellingsen, Washington State (AP-3, UP-3)
- Buddy Dial, Rice (INS-2, UP-3)

Tackles

Alex Karras, Iowa (AAB, AP-1, FWAA, INS-1, NEA-1, SN, UP-1, Time, WC)

- **Lou Michaels**, Kentucky (AAB, AFCA, AP-1, FWAA, INS-2, NEA-1, SN, UP-1, Time, WC)
- Charlie Krueger, Texas A&M (AP-2, FWAA, INS-1, UP-2)
- Tom Topping, Duke (FWAA, AP-3)
- Bob Reifsnyder, Navy (AP-2, UP-2)
- Jim McCusker, Pitt (AP-3, INS-2, UP-3)
- Bill Leeka, UCLA (INS-2)
- Larry Whitmire, Rice (INS-2)
- Nick Mumley, Purdue (INS-2)
- Dick Klein, Iowa (UP-3)

Guards

- **Bill Krisher**, Oklahoma (AAB, AP-1, FWAA, INS-1, NEA-1, SN, UP-1, Time, WC)
- **Al Ecuyer**, Notre Dame (AP-2, INS-1, SN, Time, UP-1, WC)
- Aurealius Thomas, Ohio State (AAB, AFCA, AP-1, FWAA, INS-2, UP-2)
- Bill Johnson, Tennessee (FWAA, NEA-1, AP-3, UP-3)
- Jackie Simpson, Mississippi (AFCA, FWAA, AP-2)
- Roy Hord, Jr., Duke (INS-2, UP-2)
- Stan Renning, Montana (INS-2)
- Don Wilson, Texas (INS-2)
- Joe Palermo, Dartmouth (AP-3, UP-3)

Centers

- **Dan Currie**, Michigan State (AAB, AFCA, AP-1, FWAA, INS-1, UP-2, Time, WC)
- Bob Reifsnyder, Navy (AFCA [tackle], FWAA, NEA-1)
- Don Stephenson, Georgia Tech (AP-3, INS-2, SN, UP-1)
- Bob Harrison, Oklahoma (AP-2)
- Charlie Brueckman, Pittsburgh (INS-2, UP-3)
- Jim Kernan, Army (INS-2)

Quarterbacks

- **King Hill**, Rice (AAB, AFCA, AP-1, FWAA, UP-3, Time)

- Lee Grosscup, Utah (AP-2, FWAA, INS-2, NEA-1, UP-2)
- Tom Forrestal, Navy (INS-1, AP-3, UP-2)
- Jim Van Pelt, Michigan (INS-2)
- Bob Newman, Washington State (INS-2, UP-3)

Backs

- **John David Crow**, Texas A&M (AAB, AFCA, AP-1, FWAA, INS-1, NEA-1, SN, UP-1, Time, WC)
- **Walt Kowalczyk**, Michigan State (AFCA, AP-2, FWAA, INS-2, NEA-1, SN, AFCA, UP-1, Time, WC)
- **Bob Anderson**, Army (AP-2, FWAA, INS-1, NEA-1, SN, UP-1, Time, WC)
- **Clendon Thomas**, Oklahoma (AFCA, INS-2, SN, UP-1, WC)
- Jim Pace, Michigan (AAB, AP-1, INS-2, UP-2)
- Dick Christy, North Carolina State (AAB, AP-1)
- Bob Stransky, Colorado (AP-2, FWAA, INS-1, UP-3)
- **Jim Bakhtiar,** Virginia (FWAA, AP-3)
- **Jim Taylor,** LSU (FWAA, AP-3)
- Don Clark, Ohio State (INS-2, UP-2)
- Jim Shanley, Oregon (INS-2)
- Billy Stacy, Mississippi State (INS-2)
- Reddy Osborne, Texas A&M (INS-2)
- Wray Carlton, Duke (INS-2)
- Bobby Mulgado, Arizona State (AP-3)
- **Nick Pietrosante**, Notre Dame (UP-3)
- College All stars 1957-58

| August 15, 1958 | **College All-Stars**[6]35 | | Detroit Lions | 19 | 70,000 | NFL 15–8–2 |

MVP's

| 1958 | Bobby Mitchell | Halfback/Wide receiver | Illinois |
| | Jim Ninowski | Quarterback | Michigan State |

CHAPTER 7

-WELCOME TO GREEN BAY-

Danny

When I first pulled into Green Bay after playing in the All Star game, I was driving into a town of about 52,000 people and it was like going from riches to rags.

Remember, I grew up in Detroit, went to school just outside the capital of the state of Michigan (East Lansing) and I wasn't used to a town this size. Besides I had been living somewhat of a celebrity's life, in front of the cameras on the Perry Como and

Ed Sullivan shows. I was the subject of many interviews, posing for photos in New York, Detroit, Chicago and Honolulu. After all, I was Dan Currie, *the number one college player in the nation* and the number three overall pick. I went in the first round to the Green Bay Packers. Along with me they also got Jerry Kramer, Jim Taylor and Ray Nitschke and many say it was the best draft in NFL history.

Jerry Kramer and Me in 1958

Lombardi hadn't seen us yet.

I didn't know a soul in Green Bay and I felt very awkward and out of place there. Of course, Green Bay was a professional football town and their team had been around a lot of a lot longer than Dan Currie.

By the time I reported to camp in the summer of 1958, the team was pretty much straightened out with its personnel. The head coach, Scooter McLean, put me at linebacker behind Carlton Massey who had been an All Pro at Cleveland and who had just joined the team.

I was in top physical shape and the guys like Paul Hornung helped make my welcome a cordial one. I guess it was natural to start hanging around with the other rookies, like Jerry Kramer, Jim Taylor and my old enemy from my college days, Ray Nitschke. They were trying Ray out at middle linebacker and me at strong side linebacker.

For the first half of the season, I was playing on one platoon and I damn near cried. I was really frustrated. In the opening game against the Bears, all I could ask myself was, "How bad of a football player am I that Scooter wouldn't put me on *all* the platoons?"

I know I sound contrary, but I disputed many things McLean did as a coach, but needless to say, the fact that we ended up with 1-10-1 record that season makes me feel I was more right than wrong about him.

There was no doubt that my rookie year was a big letdown after the good years at Michigan State and all the national publicity I had received during those years. I thought of all those moments of glory especially on nights when I couldn't sleep, thinking how awful I must be. I thought of all those bowl games, being a team leader, and of Perry Como, Ed Sullivan, and the bright spotlights and recognition.

At Michigan State there was a sharp organization and up in Green Bay the club was run like an outhouse. There seemed to be no master plan or direction.

When a team doesn't do well, most of the fans automatically look to the players, but I differ with that type of thinking. To me, any team that doesn't do well on the field is the result of inadequate planning by management.

The only way one gets through a 1-10-1 season is by staying together as a team and there was a bunch of great guys who stuck together and my attitude started to improve after I became a starting linebacker when Carlton Massey broke his leg.

The first contact I had with Vince Lombardi was when we played the New York Giants in an exhibition game in Boston. We beat the hell out of them. 47-10. Max McGee caught four touchdown passes and we blew the Giants right out of the stadium, yet one of the things Lombardi told us when he came to Green Bay a year later was:

"You guys are nothing but a bunch of stumble bums and the only way you're going to survive is because of me."

This is one of many pictures.   (1960)

(Brown County Arena in background)

We sometimes wore each other's gear.

This was Paul Hornung's cape - #5.

We're figuring out

"what the hell's going on out there."

Zeke, on the phone, telling Bart what we think.

GOT MILK?

This is how we got it - FREE!

Back-Jess Whittenton, John Symack, Emlen Tunnell, Hank Gremminger

Front –Bill Forrester, Bill Quinlan, Dave Hanner, John Roach, Henry Jordan, Willie Davis, Dan Currie,

CHAPTER 8

- A Collection of Fine Young Men –

There was no question that we had a lot of talent around. I could see Bart Starr, a shy, thoughtful and dedicated guy as a leader whom everyone respected. Jerry Kramer and I, draft mates and roommates, and Ray Nitschke, who at that time, was hell on wheels in more ways than one.

Max McGee was one heck of a receiver and Jim Taylor was as

hard as anyone I had ever seen. I had known Paul Hornung when we played against him at Notre Dame. He was a quarterback then, but was now a running back. I knew that we were not a 1-10-1 team. No way!

I had 20 credits to pick up so I went back to Michigan State when the disastrous 1958 season ended. This involved my student teaching which I carried out and got my degree in education.

Mary, the kids and I went back to Green Bay in early June. I could have done one of two things; hang around the golf course all day, play 18 holes and then get full of beer or get a job. I had two small children at the time. So here I was with my degree in education but I went to work for Green Bay Foods packing pickles. One of my fellow co-workers was Vince Lombardi, Jr. The job served to get me in shape and defray the outflow of gold.

I'd heard that Hornung and McGee had reported to camp, dropped their bags off in their room and split for town. When Lombardi found out he flew into a rage. He had someone go into town and haul their asses back to camp. He told them that if they didn't like it here, to forget about unpacking and leave town. I must say that it didn't seem to bother either Paul or Max very much. They went to their rooms and then showed up for practice like everyone else and that was that. Not another word was said about it.

In those days, our exhibition season was conducted much differently that it is today, mostly for economic considerations. We went east for a couple of games and ended up staying in Bear Mountain on the Hudson River.

We had flown in from the west coast and had played the New York Giants up in Bangor, Maine and we were going to be at Bear Mountain for one week to prepare for another pre-season game.

On Sunday, Vince had the priest come in to say an early Mass up at our resort hotel. It was big resort area but had no Catholic Church in the vicinity. We joked about Vince "having a pipeline to the Pope" to get this kind of service but we never said that in front of him. He took his faith seriously and when you were around him you took yours the same way.

Mass was set to begin at 7:30 A.M. and that meant you were there by 7:15 by Lombardi's clock. Hornung, McGee and I showed up and a few vacationers were also stepping inside the makeshift chapel.

Because we wanted Vince to see us, we moved up to the front seats, and just as we sat down who should appear in a black cassock and white surplus but the most celebrated altar boy in the country -- Vince Lombardi -- who genuflected and lit the candles with the greatest aura of piety.

I couldn't help but turn around and get the reaction from the other people in attendance. Vince's presence up there, kneeling and serving Mass, gave everyone a great sense of humility. I know it did me. Here was the "Leader of the Band" and the "Captain of the Ship," serving

Mass and it caused one to take stock of one's self.

-

TO OPEN THE 1959 REGULAR SEASON, the Green Bay Packers astounded everyone by putting together three straight wins.

Then we traveled to Milwaukee with our 3-0 record to face the Los Angeles Rams and they beat the hell out of us, 41-7. Toward the end of the game, Emlen Tunnell, our veteran cornerback, who Lombardi had brought with him from the Giants, came into our huddle and said:

"Gentlemen, it doesn't look like it's our day but there's

not a hell of a lot we can do about it. The simplest and easiest thing we can do is shut up, play the game as best we can and get the hell out of town."

Well, this was a far cry from the year before when everybody would be blaming everybody else each time an opponent's touchdown was scored and chaos would reign everywhere on the field and on the sidelines.

Now with Emlen, he held our secondary together really well, and the fact he had played with the New York Giants made him a winner in our eyes and he brought more than little class to 'lil' old Green Bay.

We were 3-4 after losing four in a row and were set to play the Redskins in Green Bay. Before the game we were all apprehensive about what Coach Lombardi would say to us but he surprised us saying:

"Gang, we've been playing good football and I have no complaints about the way you've been playing. A couple of things just haven't gone our way. Let's continue to play the type of ball we've been playing and it'll turn around for us."

After that statement of confidence from Coach Lombardi, we lost only one more game the rest of the season and ended with a 7-5 record.

The interesting thing about that first year under Vince was that in four of the games we lost, Jimmy Taylor. He didn't play. He had spilled hot grease on his foot in a fluke accident.

Jim's wife had dropped a big iron frying pan in the kitchen and Jimmy rushed in to help, but instead of throwing a wet towel over the smoking, hot pan, he tried to pick it up and it spilled hot grease all over his foot and burned his hand.

Conceivably, with Jimmy in the line-up we could have won the division in Lombardi's first year.

Under Vince, a team party became a ritual after the final game of the season. In December 1959, we were on the west coast having just beaten the Rams.

We had a big party and the champagne flowed, thanks to Vince. We felt good and drank toasts to our coach. We had worked hard, played good football and we finally were *together* and a confident bunch of guys.

On the last night out there before we boarded the train for

Wisconsin, I met a guy who owned several restaurants around Los Angeles. He had gone to Michigan State and he gave me three fifths of booze and I packed them away. Although it was kind of a Christmas gift, I felt it might come in handy on the long train ride home.

Several of the guys, including Fuzzy Thurston, Ron Kramer and Jesse Whittenton started up a card game in the galley. They were sitting with their sunglasses on and before I left I told Fuzzy about the three bottles in my bag and to help himself if he and the other guys wanted a nip. My duffle bag was in the closet off the galley.

About an hour later, I went back there and they were still playing cards. The atmosphere was bright and they still had on their sunglasses. Fuzzy lifted up his coffee cup and acknowledged me and I knew he had gotten into my bag in the closet.

Lombardi walked in unexpectedly and started sniffing.

"You guys are acting kind of goofy and I smell something," he said in that deep voice of his. He looked around and all the guys sat there with their coffee cups in their hands but no one said a word.

"Is anyone drinking here?" he asked.

I put my arm around him and before he could start sniffing the coffee cups up close and I said, "Vincent, you're the one who bought 120 bottles of champagne last night. You know what it's like. You have a couple of glasses of water or coffee the next morning after all that champagne and you feel a little tipsy."

"Yeah, yeah that sounds about right, Danny. But I tell you one thing. No more of that champagne from now on."

And then he walked out and I thought I caught him smiling a little.

1961 NFL World Championship at Green Bay
Dec. 31, 1961: PACKERS 37, Giants 0
Jim Taylor, Dan Currie, Vince Lombardi, Dave Hanner.

What a great day for Green Bay!

(Courtesy of the Green Bay Packers)

- Our Changing Fortunes -

On December 31, 1961 the Green Bay Packers were World Champions!

We blew out the New York Giants, in Green Bay, 37-0, and now the entire team had adjourned to the Mayfair Lounge in downtown Green Bay, next to the Northland Hotel.

When I walked in the door, Jerry Kramer handed me a full bottle of champagne.

Bart Starr was in the middle of the stage and Lou Carpenter was playing the drums. Lou had a cigarette dangling from the corner of his mouth and was having a ball. Someone in the crowd handed him a can of beer, which he grabbed with one hand, drank it down and never lost the beat or removed the cigarette from his mouth.

As the music went on and one and got louder and louder, Bart was trying to calm things down a little by introducing the players.

There was a massive crowd accumulating and the management was having a hell of a time moving people out the back door in order to let other people in the front.

Finally, Bart got the quiet he needed and he introduced Emlen

Tunnell, who came on stage and recited a poem to the audience.

Then Bart called on our young back-up quarterback, John Roach, who had managed to get into the game in the last minute or two. Roach was a quite a little drunk and slurred his words and said, "Ladies and Gentlemen, I made $5,000 today…sitting on my ass."

The crowd went wild and cheered John as he weaved and hiccupped his way off the stage.

We were a happy bunch of guys. World Champions! And now, twice -- Western Division champions and this was only Lombardi's third year.

-

In 1962, we repeated as the World Champions, beating the New York Giants again; this time in New York with a score of 17-7.

After the game, Frank Gifford sent a limousine over to our hotel to pick up Paul Hornung, Max McGee and myself and take us to a party.

Frank Gifford was one of the fair-haired guys in the Big Apple and was one of the centers of attention at the party and there were a

number of other Giants players around as well.

You knew who the Giants players were because all the beautiful women were around *them.*

Paul, Max and I stood in the corner like dummies, watching all the action.

As another lovely creature floated by us to fawn over one of the Giants players, Paul asked, "Who in hell *won* the championship today, anyway?"

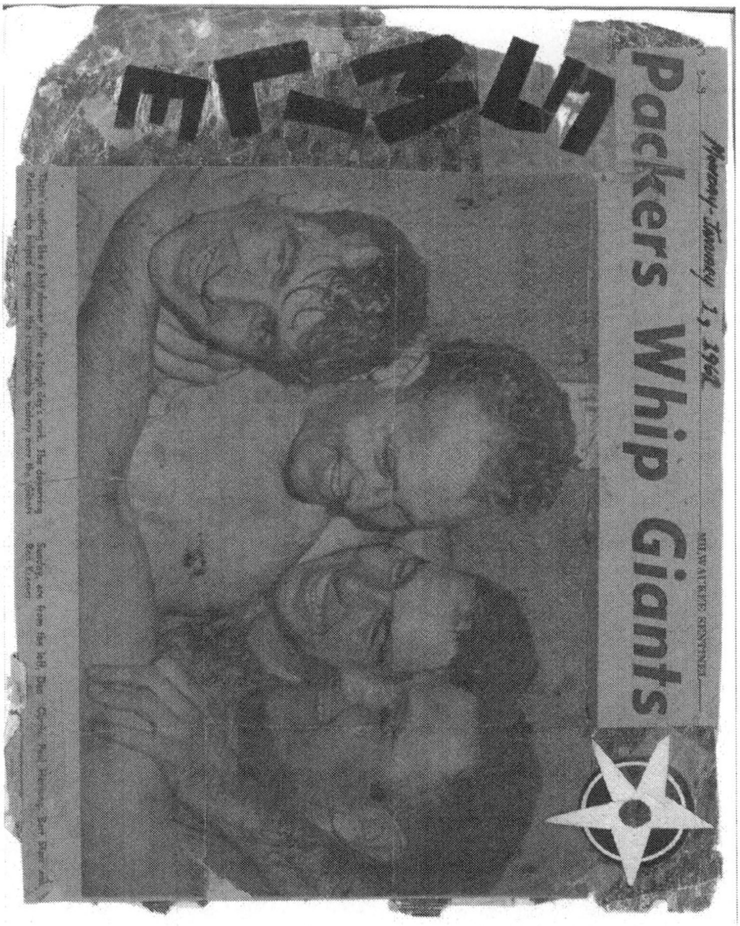
MILWAUKEE SENTINEL
Packers Whip Giants

CHAPTER 9

- Not the Greatest Position to Play -

- Let's Backtrack A Little-

In 1959, I was elected the player representative of the Green Bay Packers. For the six years following I found that it put me in a very precarious position with management.

I had heard that our NFL Player Association president, Kyle Rote, was having some difficulties with the Giants management. In fact, when Kyle had organized the association, there was at least one player rep, Redskins' quarterback Eddie LeBarron, who came to meetings but the Redskins never allowed him to be identified or to be photographed with other player reps.

Two of the veteran Packers, Jimmy Ringo and Dave Hanner, talked me into taking the job. I felt it was a great honor but I had no idea what some of the duties would be and at the time and little did I know there would be times I would have to jeopardize my position as a player.

In the first crisis I had to negotiate with management -- which meant the general manager and the head coach, Vince Lombardi was about the seating arrangements for the players' wives at home games.

When Green Bay's new stadium had been completed in 1957, the Packers organization promised that player's tickets for wives, friends, relatives or whomever, would be around midfield. But, for the past two seasons, the players were given end zone tickets which made the wives very unhappy and in our opinion unhappy wives were not good for the players' morale.

Bob Skoronski asked me to take it up with Vincent and we invited the coach to a meeting with all the players to discuss changing the location of the seats.

"For all I know that's where my wife sits," replied Vince.

Bill Quinlan stood up and said, "I'll swap you even."

- Vince blew up!!! -

I was sitting in the back of the room and I got up immediately to try and calm things down.

I emphatically made my point.

"I understand from the players who were here before me -- and before you, too, Vince -- that management had agreed to change the seats but have done nothing about it for three years. If this is true, this tells us that you don't give a damn and that the word of the management doesn't mean a thing."

He was getting huffy and started stomping around.

"If that's going to interfere with my ball club then …"

He stopped in mid-sentence and looked at me as I started walking up to the front of the room. I was coming down the center aisle and with this arm he drew and pointed to an imaginary line.

"Don't you dare cross that line," he shouted.

"I have no intention of crossing any line, Coach, but you claim to be an honorable man which we all believe you are. You've got the ball! Change the seats and you'll never hear another word about it from now on."

It really got *hot* in that room! The guys were all grumbling and Vincent was turning bright red in the face.

This was the first confrontation. As the player representative, I had organized it, and though I thought he would eventually change the seats, I saw how difficult it was and how severely the lines were drawn between players and management.

Vince was a super disciplinarian, a super tough guy when it came to conditioning, training camp, dedication strategy and carrying out a game plan and I was convinced he was more comfortable in the role of coach than that of general manager.

I guess he couldn't relent too quickly at this first meeting because he didn't want to set any bad precedents but his own sense of fairness would be tested again and again and I would be the guy who would do the testing.

There were a number of incidents around the league at that time where free agents were coming into camp, playing in scrimmages, getting hurt and then leaving without getting paid or without having their hospital and medical bills picked up by the club.

We had a guy named Jim Temp who the Packers had waived through the league but Vince decided to play him.

He had had a serious shoulder operation and subsequently tore up his shoulder again in a pre-season game.

Management refused to pick up his medical bills and suddenly dropped him from the roster without paying him a dime.

Dave Hanner came to me and said that Jim Temp was in a bad way and he asked me to go and talk to Vince.

"There's nothing I can do, Danny. I waived Jim Temp through the league already."

"Yes, I know, but you played him after that," I said. "You have to assume some responsibility for him now, if not as coach, as the general manger."

You could see he was *hot* but he said he would pay Temp his salary and would cover the doctor bills up to that time and I thought that was fair and I left it at that.

Then we had another incident where a young man from Hillsdale College was given a tryout. He flunked his physical but for some reason had been issued equipment. It was only a few days later that he hurt his knee and it had to be operated on.

Jack Venessee, the Packers business manager said that because the kid had flunked his physical, the club could not and would not assume any of the liabilities resulting from the injury.

In other words, there would be no salary compensation and no payment of any medical bills …period.

Again I had to go to Vince to straighten out this matter. Although he never had a lot of words to say, it was my responsibility to put enough heat on him to make it uncomfortable for the two of us, and get him to talk.

As far as the kid from Hillsdale was concerned, Vince agreed to pay all his medical bills and give him half his salary. I said that would be fine and as far as I was concerned he could negotiate the salary matter with the boy personally.

Just before I left the room I told him:

"Vince, you just can't leave a guy with two kids lying there without anything coming in."

I guess I didn't have to have said that because he looked up, stared bullets at me and said nothing.

Chapter 10

- Jeopardy -

There were occasions when I was on the field when I felt because I was the Player Representative and had to force Lombardi's hand, I got my ass chewed out more than I deserved.

I am convinced that every Player Rep who is elected to that role jeopardizes his position and standing as an active player, but I am not suggesting that in this role, in any way, my pro-career with the Packers and/or afterward was shortened. It was just very uncomfortable at times.

Vince Lombardi, of course, was a great human being and there are hundreds of stories about his sincerity, dedication and achievements but he was a complex man -- tough and soft, stern and flexible, single-minded and yet, understanding.

In my experience the incident relating to Gene Brito illustrates his charitable heart and also the scope of his understanding of the human condition.

Gene Brito had been and All Pro defensive end for the Washington Redskins and the Los Angeles Rams and now had been struck with a crippling disease; a degeneration of the nervous system -- the same disease that killed Lou Gehrig. *(Ironically and sadly, years later my brother Miles would also die of Lou Gehrig's disease. ALS)*

At our player meeting, I had brought up the fact that I had been contacted by a number of Player Reps in the League and it was suggested that we donate all the *fines* money to Mrs. Brito.

Usually this money, which is collected from players' fines throughout the season, was saved until the end of the year and spent on a party for all of us.

At the time we had about $700 in our kitty and before I made any suggestions and before I got the guys together, I had talked it over with Vince.

"Gentlemen," I said, "we all know about the condition of our comrade Gene Brito, but some of you may not know how much his health is failing him. As a result, bills are piling up and his wife is struggling to pay them. I have been in contact with other teams in the league and they are donating their fine money to help Gene's family. And some of the teams have a hell of a lot in fines."

Now I knew Lombardi was standing right around the corner, listening in, so I continued:

"Before we get down to a vote, I must tell you that due to the generosity of our great head coach and astute general manager, all of the expenses of any party at the end of the season will be picked up by the Packers' front office, so, should we agree to donate our fine fund to Mrs. Brito?"

Suddenly Vince appeared from around the corner, grinning from ear to ear -- he couldn't stand it anymore, especially when I had referred to him in such glowing terms.

As he walked by me he said, "Danny, you just keep thinking that way."

Then, we unanimously voted to donate our $700 to Mrs. Brito.

-

The Season of "da Bears"

In 1963, our 11-2-1 record wasn't quite as good as the Chicago Bears 11-1-2 and they went on to win the Western Division title and defeat the New York Giants 14-10 for the World Championship.

It was the year we played without Paul Hornung, who was suspended for one year by NFL Commissioner Pete Rozelle for gambling.

We all went through a difficult time, each of us meeting with the Federal Bureau of Investigation, telling what we did or didn't know about gambling and particularly that of Paul's. There is no doubt in my mind that we would have won everything that year with him in the line-up -- he was that valuable to the team.

One day, Pat Peppler, one of the business managers of the Packers called me at home and said he wanted to talk about my contract for the 1964 season.

He started off by saying, "Well, Dan, you know you didn't have a very good year."

I blew up!

"Who the hell are you? First of all, the only guy I talk contact with is Vincent Lombardi. Furthermore, I am not even going to talk to him about it. He'll have to get in touch with my attorney."

And with that, I hung up.

Chapter 11

- Rumors Abound –
Still we played and had fun

There were rumors that floated around later that Pat Peppler had told Vince what I said and that Vince immediately put my ass on the market.

From what I understand, he almost negotiated a deal with the Redskins' Ed Breedlove, but that went by the boards. But Vince never said a word about any of this to me, even during our negotiations.

In the spring of 1964, Fuzzy Thurston promoted a Charity golf tournament in which most of the Packers and some of the wealthier Packers followers participated. It was for underprivileged boys and it was held just outside Appleton at one if the better country clubs.

Earlier that year Fuzzy had joined with a guy named Bill Martine to open a restaurant in Appleton called The Left Guard. Later, Max McGee would join in the venture with a restaurant called The Left End in Manitowoc. But, this was their first year to promote this golf tournament.

I give Fuzzy a lot of credit for putting this together and presenting this opportunity to help the kids. This was before the $25,000 Super Bowl paychecks when a lot of the guys get a big bonus and can afford to get into something for charity like this, but that was all in the future and after I had parted from the Packers organization.

The night before the charity golf tournament was to be held, we spent a lot of hours at the Left Guard and as a result, getting up in the morning was not easy.

The tournament was to be played at the beautiful North Shore

Country Club on Lake Winnebago, just outside Appleton.

My partner was Jack Keppler, Vince's close friend and confidant, and he and I were paired with Vince and Paul Hornung, who had come into town the night before.

Vince was nervous and must have looked at his watch over 50 times while were standing on the tee ready to begin the play.

I don't think Vince knew that Paul had already arrived in Wisconsin and I am sure he had not seen him yet and I knew he had doubts about whether Hornung would show up at all; which was usual for Paul.

Back and forth, back and forth; he walked the same way he did on the sidelines during the game when things were not going the way he wanted them to go.

Suddenly, he stopped...

"Danny," he said, "...if he doesn't show up in the next five minutes, we're teeing off without him. There's no telling where that crazy bastard is."

So I said, "You're calling the signals, Vince."

And just at that moment, Rick Cassares and Paul came wheeling around the corner in Paul's Cadillac and Paul jumps out, grabs his bag and runs up to the tee.

I said, "Paul, you're a very lucky man. Vinnie gave you *only* five minutes more or we were teeing off without you."

Paul looked at Vince...

"Vince," he said, "you waited a whole year for me to return. What the hell's the difference of five more minutes?"

Vince didn't know what to say. He got all flustered but he took the jab pretty well.

I couldn't help laughing as I was walking down the fairway. Vince had his head down and was shaking it back and forth and smiling.

"Paul," I said, "you got him this time."

To which Paul replied, "You, too, Danny. But, you'd better call your lawyer and have him meet us at the nineteenth hole."

Vince heard him and the smile abruptly disappeared from his face.

"SHUT UP! Let's play golf," he barked.

-

A SIDE STORY

It was 1964 -- *the year Hornung came back to play after a year's suspension for gambling.*

One day during the '64 training camp, we were sitting around and Vince excitedly addressed the team.

"I know a guy who'll give you 600 electoral votes and he'll take LBJ." *(Lyndon B. Johnson for President)*

With that Max McGee said loudly, "Yeah, and I know who that is -- it's Jack Keppler.

"You're right," Vince shot back.

Of course, Jack Keppler was Vince's friend and confidant.

Then Ray Nitschke popped up and said, "Hey, I was told you're not supposed to hang around with *gamblers*."

With that, Vince gave Ray the dirtiest goddamn look I had ever seen him give anyone.

He couldn't say another word. He scowled and jumped right into the meeting.

I told Ray to lay low because the next time *you* make a wrong move, "Vince will be all over your ass."

We all went back to The Left Guard after the tournament and needless to say, the booze flowed and flowed. We were still weeks away from reporting to training camp and there was an e*specially* good feeling about Paul being back with the boys.

I stayed at Fuzzy's house that night, as I often did when I came to Wisconsin for a visit and after partying. He had three great kids, two boys, Griff and Mark, and a darling little girl named *Victoria*. Fuzzy picked out her name right after we were victorious in the 1962 World Championship.

I was dead tired so I plopped down on Mark's bed and went out like a light. When I woke up in the morning I thought I had died and gone to heaven because I saw a full-blown picture of Rachael Welch inches above my head. When I mentioned it to Fuzzy, he said, "That's my boy! I like the way he thinks!"

With my own family -- by this time I had five kids of my own -- and there was an incident that caused my wife, Mary, great distress.

She was a deeply religious woman and she was quite upset because she caught our two boys, Thomas and Matthew, hiding pictures of strippers in their room. She said, "I want you to speak to your sons about this situation."

I calmed her down and said, "Well, Mary, we'd really have a situation if they were hiding pictures of Johnny Mathis in their room."

When I was a kid, I was caught with a picture of a stripper inside my prayer book and my mother was aghast. My father reassured her that this was normal for boys and it was not the end of the world and it was never mentioned again.

Chapter 12

- The Writing on the Wall -

One of the off-season pastimes a pro football player has is studying the draft and each year when you look at the new names coming into the game, you realize, that as a player, you're nothing more than chattel because management is constantly seeking to stock the pond.

So, in 1964, when coach acquired Dave Robinson from Penn State -- a defensive end linebacker -- a warning signal went up to our defensive ends and linebackers, of which I was one.

It was obvious that eventually, the head man, Lombardi, would get Robinson into the line-up. So, when we got to camp and Robbie was assigned to play behind me, I knew it would only be a matter of time -- one, two, three years -- before he would break into the starting line-up.

Vince had to get *his* first draft choice into that lineup, if for no other reason than to look good on paper as a top recruiter and excellent judge of talent. But, in all fairness, Robby was really, *really* good.

I was struggling, fighting, battling and clawing every bit of the way to stay in front of Robinson.

Then, one game there was a blitz situation and Robbie came in for me.

Even though it was just for that one play, I knew that I'd be traded.

You get that sick feeling weighing heavily inside of your gut and it makes you weak for a minute or two. You try to shrug it off, but you know it will come back to you; that feeling of not being *number one*.

In April 1965, we had a player's representative and owners meeting down at the Kenilworth Hotel in Miami.

This was the first time the Player Representatives and front office management had a meeting together and each player rep sat alongside his general manager or coach and everyone was handed a long list of names and their club affiliation. Pete Rozelle, the NFL Commissioner, served as moderator.

Now, Lombardi was sitting on my right and he suddenly drew a line through my name, scratching it out as the Player Representative of the Green Bay Packers.

I gave him a sharp jab with my elbow and said, "Hey, what's that bullshit?"

I guess he'd forgotten I was sitting next to him because he seemed startled.

He said, "No, no, no, no... I was just scribbling."

"Just scribbling, my ass, you scratched me out."

The meeting came to order and for the next hour or so we got involved in a discussion about pension monies and I nearly forgot about Vince's doodling but when we broke for lunch, Vince caught me in the lobby and pulled me aside, saying:

"I've got to explain something to you. Ron Kramer's gone to Detroit and I don't know how much more Max has left. I've got to get a receiver or else I'm in trouble. I've been talking to Los Angeles and they are willing to give up Carroll Dale. They want you in return, Danny."

Vince tried to smile and then he put his arm around me.

"You'll like it out there, Danny, you know that."

What a crock of bullshit!

I thought my heart was going to stop then and there. But, I heard myself thanking him and I suppose for mental survival, I suddenly I had a jumble of mental pictures in my head about the times we had played out there on the west coast and the two Pro-Bowl games I had participated in over the past seven years. I pictured the Coliseum, the Beverly Hills Hotel, beautiful looking people, the beaches -- the parties --the discotheques -- the movie studios. I could almost feel the warm glow and shine of California.

Perhaps my survival instinct was trying to make the best of the situation at that moment, but I remember looking up and catching someone's eye and he waved to me.

And then I thought, he's waving at Dan Currie, a member of the

World Champion Green Bay Packers, but, at that moment I was on my way out and there was no one there who knew it yet except Vince and me and whoever he was talking to at the Rams.

I said, "Don't worry about me, Vince. You just take care of your team. You have tough decisions to make, and I know that, and you don't need to play baby sitter for me."

I was sick to my stomach but I straightened up and just before we went back into the meeting room he told me that the deal was not yet finalized and that I shouldn't say a word to anyone.

Four days later, back in Green Bay he called me at home. The conversation was brief and the only thing that stands out in my mind are the words...**"...you are officially the property of the Los Angeles Rams."**

I said, "I want you to know coach that I enjoyed the many years under your tutelage and being part of the Green Bay Packers. The memories and the feeling will always remain with me. You made me a good football player. Please tell the rest of the staff and my teammates that I wish them all the luck in the world."

Then I hung up and that's how I became an EX-*Green Bay Packer.*

In the days that followed the announcement, I got kind of a bitter at the press and the reports that said I had had big arguments with Vince. *What bullshit!*

Perhaps this inaccurate reporting was triggered because I had hung around with Bill Quinlan who was once my roommate and who looked a lot like me. We were often misidentified and I know that Bill did have a number of run-ins with Vince, but as far as I was concerned, the coach and I had never had any major disagreements.

If a reporter had been within earshot outside the *Brenner* Hall at Saint Norbert's College, he might have noted the following:

I was limping a bit because my left knee was acting up. I knew it would be all right once the practices got underway, but right now it was sore as hell.

When Vince saw me he asked, "What wrong with the leg, Danny?"

I explained the knee operation I had back in 1951 when I was a high school freshman and that the doctors at the time, didn't know how to rehabilitate knees.

I told Him that I had suffered a degree of atrophy ever since.

Lombardi shook his head and said:

"Danny, the only atrophy you have is between your ears."

-

So, here I was. I was 29 years old, an ex-All pro, an ex-World Champion and an ex-Green Bay Packer and I suddenly had a new identity:

Dan Currie, *Los Angeles Ram.*

I think you can tell by the look on my face that I was uncomfortable in a Los Angeles Rams uniform.

Chapter 13

(With the Rams)

- A new lease on life –

To me, the West Coast meant Hollywood and not the Los Angeles Rams, but when I reported to Chapman College in San Fernando Valley in 1965, I was thrilled to be given a warm and excellent reception by both players and coaches.

Harland Savare was head coach, an immaculate dresser and a soft-spoken gentleman. He coached a fine bunch of Ram players and on the surface it looked like the team might be contenders for the Western Division title.

One of the first things that struck me, however, was the shoddy practice facilities in the training camp. I had heard that the Rams' owner, Dan Reeves, was pretty set in his thinking of how a team should be run and that Svare couldn't be blamed for the practice facilities which resembled a city recreational playing field.

This was a far cry from Green Bay where everything was now first class. Maybe it was all in my mind but you could see a certain spark was missing with the players, as if they were saying,

"Champions don't practice in places like this!"

Whatever the reason, once the season started, we just didn't have the personnel depth to compete with the Colts and the Packers, who were pre-season favorites to win the Western Division title. We found ourselves pressing a lot and whenever you do that, things fall apart most of the time. The entire team committed more errors in the first few games than we did in Green Bay in two full seasons.

On evening right in the middle of the season, Coach Savare called me at home. "Dan," he said, "I've got to bench you. I'm getting heat and I've got to go with my younger players." He was genuinely regretful and I told him to do whatever he had to do and I would make my own adjustments.

For the next three games I sat on the bench until our weak side linebacker, Cliff Livingston, got hurt. It was Bob Schelker who went to Savare and suggested trying me on the weak side.

 At Los Angeles the linebackers would flop -- weak side linebacker would always play the weak side of the formation and the strong side LB would always go to the side of the formation where the tight end was.

At Green Bay, I was the defensive left linebacker and since most offensive formations are strong right, most of my playing days were spent crushing or getting crushed by tight ends.

But now, here at Los Angeles, before I was moved to the weak side, I had lined up on the strong side for every play because of the flopping, and it had become more difficult for me, combat-wise, to compete with the tight ends as they were getting quicker and quicker, while I had lost a step or so.

But the difference here was in playing weak side linebacker and this didn't occur to me until in this game when I was rushed in for the injured Livingston.

I occurred to me that I had made a number of good plays from the weak side up in Green Bay and on the weak side in this game, I found that I didn't have to struggle my ass off. We won the game and the three or four that followed and of course, when you win, everybody looks good.

I now felt I had a new lease on life by playing the weak side where it was a hell of a lot easier ballgame. A little success had returned to me with the move to the weak side where I finished the season, but, in the game against my old teammates, the

Packers, shortly after I was back in the starting lineup, I once again realized that no position in pro football is easy.

The game was a kind of homecoming for me, and I received mixed reactions from the fans when I ran out onto the field at County Stadium in Milwaukee in a Rams' jersey.

In one of the first defensive plays of the game I slid toward the middle as Jimmy Taylor was handed the ball on a quick opener. The only way I could get a piece of him was to get my hand in front of his body.

As I went to tackle him, I caught one of his powerful legs right in the head.

WHAM!

He dropped me! It was like a fighter taking a hard blow directly on the button, but, a fighter has an advantage because he wears a rubber mouthpiece which causes his temples to flex. I had no mouthpiece and when I was hit, I flew to the ground, spread-eagle, out cold, and I'm happy I was unconscious because there I lay; Dan Currie, forever a Green bay Packer, in the middle of Milwaukee County Stadium in a LA Rams uniform. Not a pretty sight!

It took all but the last thirty seconds of the first half for me to regain my senses, but I was goofy, really goofy!

People came around and asked me how I felt and I very carefully nodded my head, but I was feeling like Jake LaMotta and/or a Carmen Basilio must have felt after taking a head shot.

My head was sore for a week. I couldn't sneeze without causing a hell of a lot of pain.

In the locker room after the game it was analyzed as a mild concussion and I wondered what in hell a massive concussion must feel like.

However, I felt much better after Dave Hanner and Henry Jordan came by the Rams locker room to see me and see how I was. Of course no Jim Taylor, (he would not have bothered) but I will never forget what those two fellows/friends did to help me feel better. I loved them for it.

But now, for the last game of the season, Green Bay was on the coast and the afternoon before the game, Jerry Kramer, my draft-mate, teammate, roommate and my good friend, gave me a call.

"Hey, Dapper, let's go have a beer," he said.

"Hey, Jerry, you know I would love to have a beer with you, but I just can't. I am scrambling for my very existence and I am not winning championships anymore. I can't look bad tomorrow. I've got to look good --somehow, some way."

"You mean your old buddy gives you a call and you won't go out and have a beer with him?"

"Jerry, I hate to refuse, but I just can't go. Please understand my position. For me, the party's over. I'm struggling to survive."

Jerry and I had been friends from the beginning of our pro-careers and it killed me to not go and meet up with him.

He told me he understood, and even though I wished he actually *could and did* understand, I knew he didn't, and after a brief little chat, we hung up, still and always friends.

In addition to starting as weak linebacker, I was assigned to play on the kickoff teams. I was doing anything they asked of me in order to stay there and to earn my salary.

Earlier in the season I had told the coaches, "Hey, let me play on the kick-offs -- I know how to get down there."

So that's where they put me.

-

And here's what happened.

ONE OF THE HIGHLIGHTS
During my time in LALA Land

...

A little story about Fuzzy and Me

Fuzzy was notorious for openly showing his affection to his teammates. When I was traded to the L.A. Rams for Carroll Dale in 1965, I missed everyone; especially Fuzzy Thurston and his raucous,

loving self. I mean it, I really missed him.

I loved Fuzzy and apparently Fuzzy loved me!

When the Packers kicked off against the Rams in the Los Angeles Coliseum in the fall of 1965, Fuzzy arranged to be on the field for the kick-off.

He knew I would be on the kick-off team for the Rams and so, when the whistle blew and we started the game, I could see Fuzzy charging down the field, coming right at me.

He knocked me down and jumped on top of me and then

he tore off my helmut and smothered me with kisses in front of thousands of people.

I wiggled, giggled and hollered,
"Get off me, Fuzzy, come on...what are you doing? Get off me!"

We got up and we hugged and I'm sure that whoever saw us wondered what in hell was going on, but, we laughed and laughed
and we didn't give a damn who saw us and my heart was full.

-

-

I didn't want anyone to say I sandbagged or anything else that would be detrimental to my name when I walked away from the Rams organization -- and it was readily dawning on me that it wouldn't be too much longer before I took that walk.

It was like the final curtain was about to fall -- And a sick feeling filled my stomach.

Chapter 14

- STILL HOPING -

In 1966 George Allen replaced Harland Svare as the head coach for the Rams. He frequently came over and confided and conferred with me. I suppose this came out of respect since we had once played against one another when he was coaching for the Chicago Bears.

One of the first things he asked me was what I thought about the LA Rams organization. I frankly told him that the Rams had not been disciplined enough over a period of time to put five or six wins together. It seemed to me that after a win or two they would get cocky and a little too confident and blow the next game.

Another thing I brought up to Allen when he first arrived was the sub-par, lackluster, physical training camp facilities. As I mentioned, we had practiced in a small park and recreation area in the San Fernando Valley the year before. I didn't blame this on Harland Svare and I mentioned how Dan Reeves had his own economic ideas as to how to run a football organization, but this facility was certainly a long way from being what a professional, high-caliber training site should be.

It looked "sandlot" and I think this contributed to our playing "sandlot" football at times.

When Allen finally took a look at the facilities he said to me, "Danny, you must have been appalled coming from Green Bay and that top-rated professional operation – that physical giant; the buildings, the offices, the locker rooms and the training tables which you were used to…"

He was right but I told him I wasn't about to make waves and tell *anyone* how to run their organization.

But I did say, "As you are well aware, George, if you're dressed in a good suit, you'll act like you're dressed in a good suit and if you're wearing Bermuda shorts you behave that way."

Allen knew what I was talking about and right after that conversation he told me the team was moving to Blair Field in Long Beach -- that's where the Chicago Cubs practiced in the winter -- and it now became the home of the Rams.

Blair Field was a converted baseball field with concrete stands and very conducive to private practices. It was darn nice!

Thus, George Allen's first training camp gave the team an appearance of being truly professional and one that was preparing to win a championship.

Allen of course was an excellent disciplinarian but in a much *different* way than Lombardi. Lombardi didn't always explain and/or show us the respect we felt we were entitled to, but George laid out plans to show you where you were going -- the championship -- and he was such a good salesman and organizer that everybody believed him.

And we started winning.

I am still #58 (see me on the left)

- About Great Coaches -

Allen made some good trades, acquiring such leaders as Roger Brown, Tommy Mason and GB's Hank Gremminger. Most successful coaches are basically organizers and have an uncanny ability to be damn good horse traders.

At Green Bay, Lombardi made some draft choices and trades that were phenomenal – Henry Jordan, Willie Davis, Bill Quinlan, Herb Adderley. George Allen did the same thing --- he got Jack Pardee out of retirement, traded for Maxie Baum, got Myron Padios and many others.

I remember when I was a kid, marveling at some of the trades made by Paul Brown, the first of the great horse traders. Like all great coaches to follow me in my lifetime -- Duffy Daugherty, Vince Lombardi and George Allen -- they all had the ability to look at a "horse" and know if it was going to end up in the winning circle or not.

That one *instinctive* ability separates them from the rest of the coaching pack.

-
_____

I was getting along fine with Allen and I felt he couldn't afford to get rid of me because I had been in so many championship games and I had helped him out with getting the Rams settled in a first class training facility.

I helped him out in practices. I knew how practices were to be conducted and I assisted in every way I could to make the practices go smoothly.

If in a situation when a coach needs a guard, you're the guard; if he needs a tackle, you're the tackle. Whatever happens you don't slow down the tempo of the practice – it's a show; a production that has to work.

I understood this and by helping out wherever one can you

become more and more valuable to the organization and that was one of the factors which contributed to George and I getting along as well as we did.

I guess I was doing all this because I knew the handwriting was on the wall. I called my wife, Mary, and told her what was happening, how sick I felt and that things were about to change. She was great because she always knew this day would come and she was very kind and understanding.

My left knee was in bad shape and I had to have the fluid drained out of it at least once a game. The doctor was taking three ounces or 90cc's out each time he drilled the needle into my knee cap and the medial cartilage made it so I could hardly move it.

I wound up at the University of Michigan Medical Center in Ann Arbor for the operation after the 1966 season. Dr. Bally from Saint Joseph's Hospital did the operation and put my left leg in a cast from the hip to the foot for five weeks.

Dr. Bally told me they took out large amounts of calcium deposits and that they chiseled off the top of my tibia to ease the pressure and pain because my knee had become extremely arthritic due to the torn cartilage and the pieces of calcium floating around.

I thought I had rehabilitated my knee pretty well, but when I got to the Rams training camp I knew it wasn't functioning the way it should.

Coach Allen quickly sized up my condition and told me to stay out of whatever drills -- agility drills, running ropes, etc. -- that would aggravate the knee. He told me to work it enough and he was sure it would eventually be in good shape. But it didn't happen that way!

One morning, when we were staying down in Long Beach, the

phone rang. My roommate was Claude Crab and when he handed me the receiver he said it was Joe Sullivan, George Allen's right hand man, and that George wanted to talk to me.

I knew the final curtain was falling and a sick feeling filled my stomach during the 15 minute drive to the little coffee shop where I was to meet Coach Allen.

He came right to the point and asked me what I wanted to do. I shook my head that I simply didn't know. He said there were a few teams interested in me but I told him I wasn't interested in starting all over with somebody else. He said that if I were waived through the league, he'd keep me on the taxi squad.

Since I didn't want to go back to Detroit just yet, I reconciled myself that being on the Rams taxi squad would give me a year to look around the Coast for something. I just couldn't see myself in the old factory town of Detroit, except that my family was there and I would have to talk that over with Mary.

But one thing was clear:

THE SHOW WAS OVER.

Chapter 15

-TRYING TO ACCEPT REALITY-

Since a young age I had been very fortunate in athletics, but let's face it, football is a young man's game and all that early glory is very hard for foolish fellows like me to give up.

Some of my teammates chided me for going to LA piano bars and singing the show tunes which I have always loved so much and enjoy performing and they were probably right.

They thought I should get a job -- a real job. But I would always turn it around on them and say, "Why don't *YOU* get a job?"

I wanted to sing!

My older brother Miles has six girls and one son and while they were still at home he had organized them into a musical group of excellent talented songsters. They might be on different floors of the house but eventually, all would chime in and harmonize to a song which Miles had started.

This was the way our folks had raised us -- *singing around the house --* and I was comfortable with this kind of expression and saw no reason not to sing whenever I could.

When I was a teenager and was taking care of my mother (She was an invalid for many years. She had developed a brain tumor as a result of my brother being shot and killed at age 16), I would sing to her and she loved it and I loved it, too, because it pleased her so much.

Sure I was hoping I might be good enough that some Hollywood pro might discover me – Dan Currie, the movie star *(maybe)*. I had been blessed with Rock Hudson looks which had probably sourced from my mother's side of the family -- she was a knockout when she was young.

I realized that my appearance was a special gift and I was hungry for more fame and fortune, so I tried to capitalize on my looks and talent.

I acted on a couple of television shows, like Jack Webb's, "Dragnet" and I also did a Texaco commercial which gave me a check for $12,000 which I immediately sent home to Mary. That was some really sweet pay in the mid-1960's.

I hung around LA for awhile and I suppose I just could not admit it was all over and instead of realizing it had simply come to a "natural" end, as it should have, I refused to believe it and besides, and mostly, I was at a loss as to which way to go.

Earlier, I had not given my life after football much of a thought and I so felt that this stage of my life was a defeat, like losing a big game, and I was *never* one to accept defeat gracefully.

Coach Shada, Duffy Dougherty, Vince Lombardi and all my other coaches had trained me well -- to accept nothing but winning.

But to win, I had to be in the game and I couldn't admit I wasn't -- anymore.

CHAPTER 16

- The years that followed after football were not only strange and difficult, but tragic -

In 1969, Mary and I got a divorce. It was unheard of in my close-knit Detroit Catholic community, especially with six kids.

I won't make excuses for myself because I am entirely to blame for our split. I had been an absentee husband and father for many years. I was always looking for "lightning in a bottle," for that instant luck which some people speak of and I believed that since good fortune had smiled on me so often before, it could happen to me again and when it did -- then I would be able to shower my wife and family with the abundance they deserved.

I missed all of my family, especially my kids, and I wanted to see them but I was never very good at taking criticism.

I had too much pride and stubbornness for going home to face the music which I would surely face there. At the time, it did not seem I had a choice. I believed the entire community would look down their noses at me, leaving me vulnerable and feeling guilty. Was I hiding? Was

I a failure? How could I be? But, was I?

I can honestly say I am sorry for being so prideful. I regret it. I did not try hard enough and, to my sorrow, it is now too late to make amends to my children but I am going to try.

Funny and sad to note, what harm early fame and the vanity and ego which comes with it, can do to a person and affect their decisions.

I often wonder how many other star athletes this has happened to, although I think young athletes today are better prepared and are tutored in how to avoid the pitfalls of the sudden success of the profession -- like how to deal with the wrong women, the attention, the money and the celebrity.

In my days and nights I have seen many of my peers succumb to alcohol, drugs, serious trouble and premature death and I, too, face many demons.

The life and health of an athlete after football is precarious. We take a hell of a beating. I was often asked why I accepted a measly few hundred dollars in monthly retirement pay from the NFL at age 55. Some said that age 55 was way too early.

I was told that if I waited until age 60 or 62, I would get a substantially larger amount and that's true. But you see -- back in my day -- the actuarial for a linebacker was 58 years of age.

Ray Nitschke was 62 when he had a massive coronary and died suddenly -- and if you recall our great tackle, Henry Jordan, died suddenly at age 42 of the same.

Both were defensive players like me, so I took my pension as early as I could get it and besides, I needed the money.

There are a couple of ladies who have been wonderful to me and with whom I am great friends, and although I came very close to tying the knot with one of them, I decided I didn't have a whole lot to offer her, and so, I passed it up and never married again.

Chapter 17

- The Twilight of my Life –

2009 – Age 74 and on

I am in my 70's now and I've retired after spending 25 years at the Stardust Hotel in Las Vegas.

No, I was not a manager or executive -- I was a night security guard. But actually, I chose this job because I wanted my days free to pursue other avenues and to spend daytime hours with my buddies.

I have a lot of trouble with my legs, which is a result of standing on my feet for so many years and this is a sign of congestive heart failure although my doctors have not diagnosed this yet.

I also have trouble standing up straight. My back has given me some problems as well as my knee. But as Vince suggested -- it's all between my ears. Hmmmm! He could be right, of course. I exercise as best I can and I eat right -- and, what the hell, I am still alive!

Once in awhile I see Jerry Kramer, Fuzzy and Hornung and when I do we have a great time reminiscing -- but we all know there is something missing -- it isn't quite the same -- it isn't the way it should be.

I know they shake their heads and wonder and probably talk about why I ended up at the Stardust Hotel, but I had to work somewhere and the Stardust hired me and was good to me.

-

I understand that football is a business and Vince did what he thought was best but I wonder where any of the guys would have ended up if Vince had traded them right before Super Bowl I.

I have always felt as though my Packers teammates are my brothers and all of my *real* brothers are dead now. As I wrote earlier, Archie, my oldest brother was shot and killed at age 16. Miles died after a long-time suffering from Lou Gehrig's disease and my youngest brother, Michael, died when a crane on a construction site fell and crushed him.

My daughter, Julie, died from a seizure a few years ago and my wife, Mary, is gone also, dying from cancer of the brain at an early age -- too early for all of them. Mary was a wonderful woman -- and no doubt is a saint in heaven.

In 1958, when I was brought to Green Bay as the number one pick of the Packers, my fellow draftees, Jerry Kramer, Ray Nitschke and all the others became my family, too. I loved them then and still do.

Each and every member of that team knew what the other was giving to make all of us World Champions. We did it together and we are ALL part of something really BIG that happened

I know what a contribution my talent was to the Packers and it was Vince Lombardi, his coaching staff and my teammates who made me a great player.

I know I was an important part of the effort which turned the Green Bay Packers into a winning machine in the '60's and which started the Packers dynasty.

I know I helped make it what it is today and I am proud of this accomplishment and I was very honored when I was inducted into the Green Bay Packers Hall of Fame in 1984, but I wish I could have stayed around much longer and been a bigger part of the glory which finally came to all those deserving Packers, my buddies.

I did not want to leave Green Bay and I guess I can say I have never really gotten over my trade to the Rams.

My trade was for me – a great loss. Almost like a death blow. It was the loss of my Packers brothers. It didn't end up the way it should have -- with me as part of it all.

Though some may say it was only a "roll of the dice," which I guess it was, in retrospect, trading me to the Rams was unnecessary.

Sure, the Pro Hall of Famer, Dave Robinson was lined up to replace me and so at the time it seemed like a good idea to Vince, but, he told me the reason I was traded was because he needed another receiver since he doubted Max McGee could play much longer.

He traded me for receiver, Carroll Dale. I doubt he truly believed this about Max or was it the reason, and as we all soon learned, and Vince learned also, McGee still had a lot left in him. Just take a look at his performance in Super Bowl I, if you don't believe me. What a champion -- Max!

I think my teammates quietly believe I should have been there with them -- even though they don't say so -- and that I should have been a Super Bowl Champion and a Lombardi Legend, too.

I guess it sounds sort of *corny* to think of myself as a *forgotten and/or missing* Lombardi Legend.

Oh, yes, that does sound *corny* and it also sounds like self-pity; egotistical and presumptuous.

So, I'll simply think of myself as:

DAN CURRIE

- GREEN BAY PACKER –

I'll always be a Packer.

I left my heart in Lambeau Field.

Dan Currie

Born: June 26, 1935

Died: September 11, 2017

Age 82

A poem by Henry Scott Holland (1847-1918)

Death is nothing at all.
I have only slipped away to the next room.
I am I and you are you.
Whatever we were to each other,
that, we still are.

Call me by my old familiar name.
Speak to me in the easy way
which you always used to.
Put no difference into your tone.
Wear no forced air of solemnity or sorrow.

Laugh as we always laughed
at the little jokes we enjoyed together.
Play, smile, and think of me. Pray for me.
Let my name be ever the household word
that it always was.
Let it be spoken without effect,
without the trace of a shadow on it.

Life means all that it ever meant.
It is the same that it ever was.
There is absolute unbroken continuity.
Why should I be out of mind
because I am out of sight?

I am but waiting for you.
For an interval,
somewhere, very near.
just around the corner.

All is well.

Love,

Danny

Starting the Diary – Madison, WI - 1971

Credits

Photo - Front Cover

From the private collection of Dan Currie

Sports Illustrated - Cover - 12/61

With Gratitude

Green Bay Packers

Cover design by Jason Lindstrum / fuse-creative.com

Some photos from the collection of Vernon Biever©

**Some photos from the private collection of
Nick Martone**

Responsibility is taken by the author for all
reproduced internet material

This book is available:
www.amazon.com
www.amazon.com/uk
www.kindle.com

Author Contact:
sssandysullivan@gmail.com

Part of the proceeds from the sale of this book will be donated to the Catholic Youth Organization of Detroit in the name of

Daniel G. Currie

PRINTED in the U.S.A

Sandy Sullivan is an author, speaker, writer, artist and lifelong Green Bay Packers fan who resides in her beautiful, beloved, home state of Wisconsin.

Made in the USA
San Bernardino, CA
17 September 2019